Birds & Butterflies

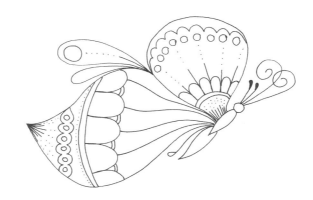

Other great books in the series

zendoodle coloring

zendoodle coloring BIG PICTURE

Tranquil Art for Experienced Eyes

Birds & Butterflies

Illustrations by Nikolett Corley

ST. MARTIN'S GRIFFIN

NEW YORK

ZENDOODLE COLORING BIG PICTURE: BIRDS & BUTTERFLIES.
Copyright © 2016 by St. Martin's Press. All rights reserved.
Printed in the United States of America. For information, address
St. Martin's Press, 175 Fifth Avenue, New York, N.Y. 10010.

www.stmartins.com

ISBN 978-1-250-12141-7 (trade paperback)

Our books may be purchased in bulk for promotional, educational, or business use.
Please contact your local bookseller or the Macmillan Corporate and Premium
Sales Department at 1-800-221-7945, extension 5442, or by e-mail
at MacmillanSpecialMarkets@macmillan.com.

First Edition: October 2016

10 9 8 7 6 5

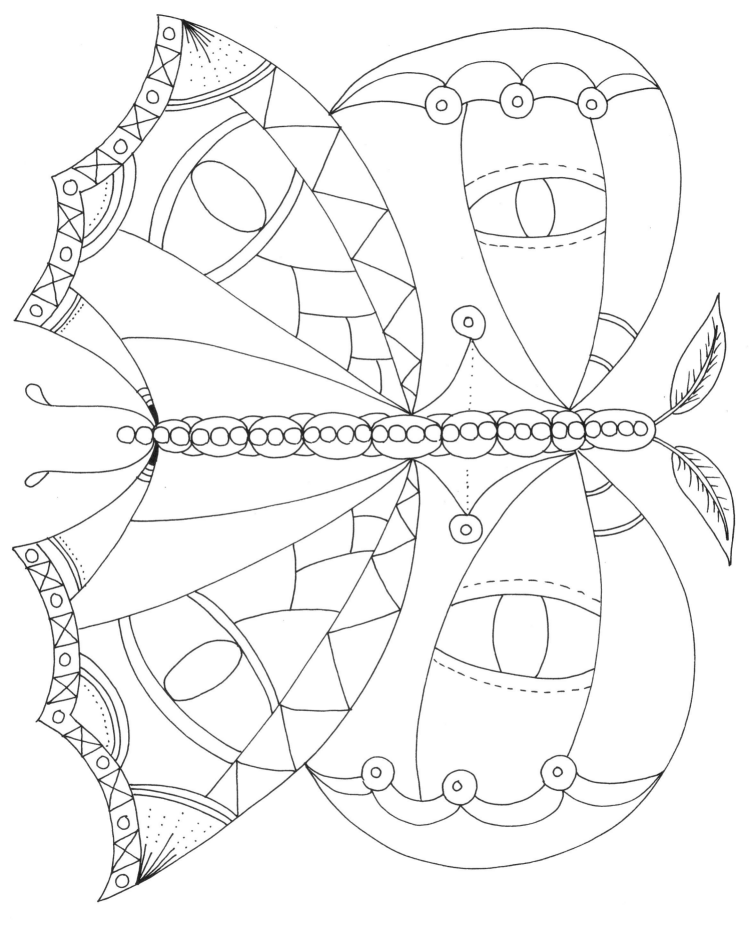

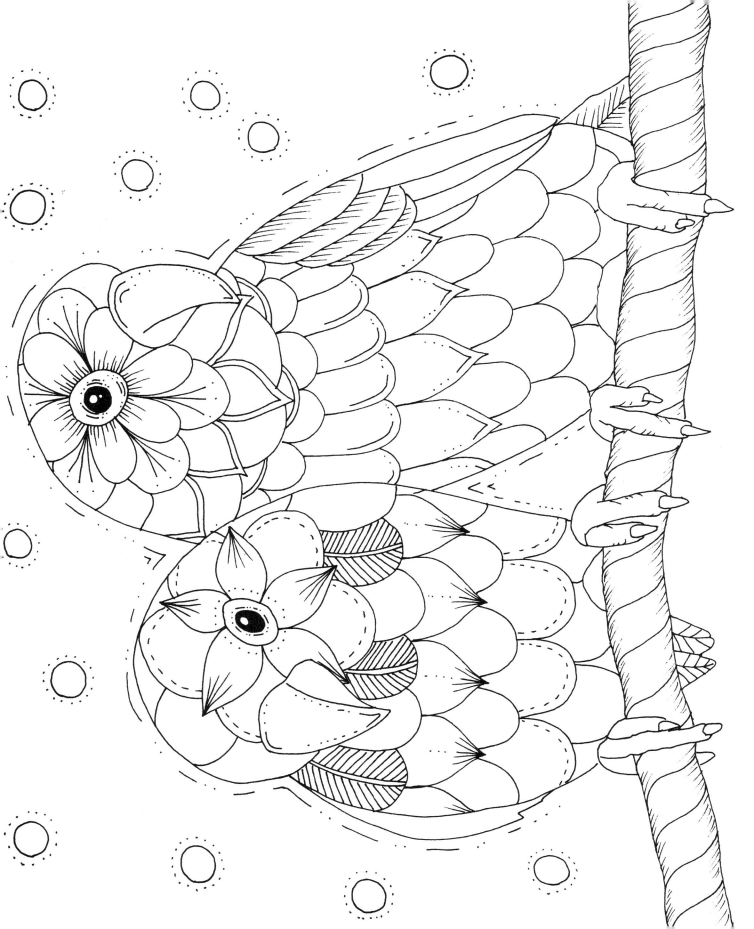

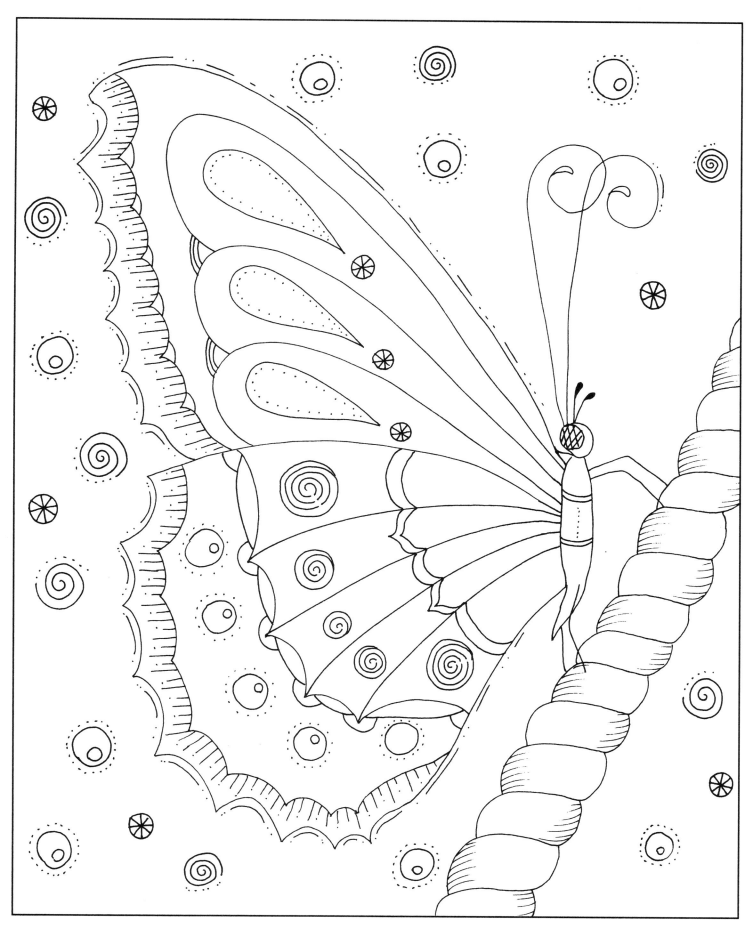